Home In These Hills
A Young Woman's Life

by Viola Coolbaugh

Altay, New York
January 1 - December 10, 1891

New York History Review Press
Elmira, New York

Home In These Hills - A Young Woman's Diary
by Viola Coolbaugh, 1891
transcribed by Diane Janowski

Copyright © 2010 Diane Janowski and photographs by Allen C. Smith
Published by New York History Review Press
Elmira, New York

Notice of Rights. All rights reserved. No part of this book may be reproduced or transmitted in any form by any means, electronic, mechanical, photocopying, recording or otherwise, without the prior written permission of the author. For more information on getting permission for reprints and excerpts, contact us through our website.
www.NewYorkHistoryReview.com

For the latest on New York History Review, please visit
www.NewYorkHistoryReview.com

All recipes are from *Our Own Book - A Victorian Guide to Life* © 2008. Courtesy of New York History Review Press.

ISBN: 978-0-578-04480-4

First Edition

Printed in the United States of America

For Orville and Orson

Viola's diary in its current condition.
Courtesy of the Eleanor Barnes Library, Elmira, New York.

Table of Contents

Foreward..8
Maps of Altay and area..10, 11
People in the Diary..12
Home In These Hills..17
New Year's Marble Cake...23
Auntie's Ginger Snaps..27
Brown Bread..33
Lemon Pie, Rhubarb Pie...36
Pork Cake..40
Cherry Pie...45
Hints for making cake..49
Silver Cake..52
Ice Cream..53
Custard Pie..56
Preserved Cherries, Homemade Soap..59
Good Girl's Cake...61
Berry Corn Cake..63
Red Raspberry Jam..64
Pickled Peaches..76
Bibiliography..81
Afterward..82

Foreword

In our *Learning from History* series of Upstate New York diaries, accounts of young people's lives on the farm, or in the home, help us to understand their thoughts and experiences. Each narrative offers a unique perspective on young peoples' lives in rural New York, and serves as an important primary resource in the study of American history.

Home in These Hills is the journal of 25-year-old Viola Coolbaugh of Altay, New York - twelve miles west of Watkins Glen, New York. Viola was born on August 24, 1865 in Altay, the daughter of Major and Susan Coolbaugh. She had an older brother named John that she did not mention in the diary, and two twin brothers Orville and Orson. In 1891 they lived on Main Street in downtown Altay.

Beginning on January 1, 1891, Viola recorded the events of her life in a small 3¼ x 4¾ inch pocket diary with two entries to the page in very nice handwriting. Viola's notations were confined to the spaces allotted and are written in pencil. Her handwriting is mostly legible, except for a few names or places that cannot be deciphered. Viola's spelling is left as she spelled it. Clarifications have been added in brackets. The photographed pages from her diary are actual size.

Viola was twenty-five years old and lived with her parents and twin brothers. She got married the following year although she did not mention having a boyfriend during this time. She had plenty of friends and neighbors. She was generally very happy in her life – she enjoyed her family, friends, and church activities. Her father owned a store in Altay on Main Street that sold baked goods, tobacco and groceries. Viola was apparently the store's baker as she constantly wrote of baking pies, cakes, cookies, and bread. We have included many old recipes of baked goods that she mentioned in her diary. She also worked many times in the Altay post office and in a local basket factory.

Home In These Hills invites us into the daily life of a New York young woman through her own words and experiences. We hear Viola's voice as she shares her joys, sorrows, enthusiasm, and fragility of life in a rural farming community.

The Eleanor Barnes Library acquired Viola Coolbaugh's diary in 2009. So far as is known, this transcription is its first published version. All of the photographs are by Allen C. Smith. All of the recipes are from *Our Own Book - A Victorian Guide to Life* from New York History Review.

Diane Janowski, Publisher

> **JELL-O PIMENTO SALAD**
>
> Dissolve a package of Lemon Jell-O in a pint of boiling water. When it begins to thicken add one cup finely chopped celery, one cup shredded cabbage, one-half green pepper, two slices pimento, one-half teaspoonful salt, one-half teaspoonful mustard, one-fourth teaspoonful paprika, two tablespoonfuls vinegar or lemon juice. Mix thoroughly. Set to harden. Serve with mayonnaise dressing.

A recipe found in the back pocket of Viola's diary.

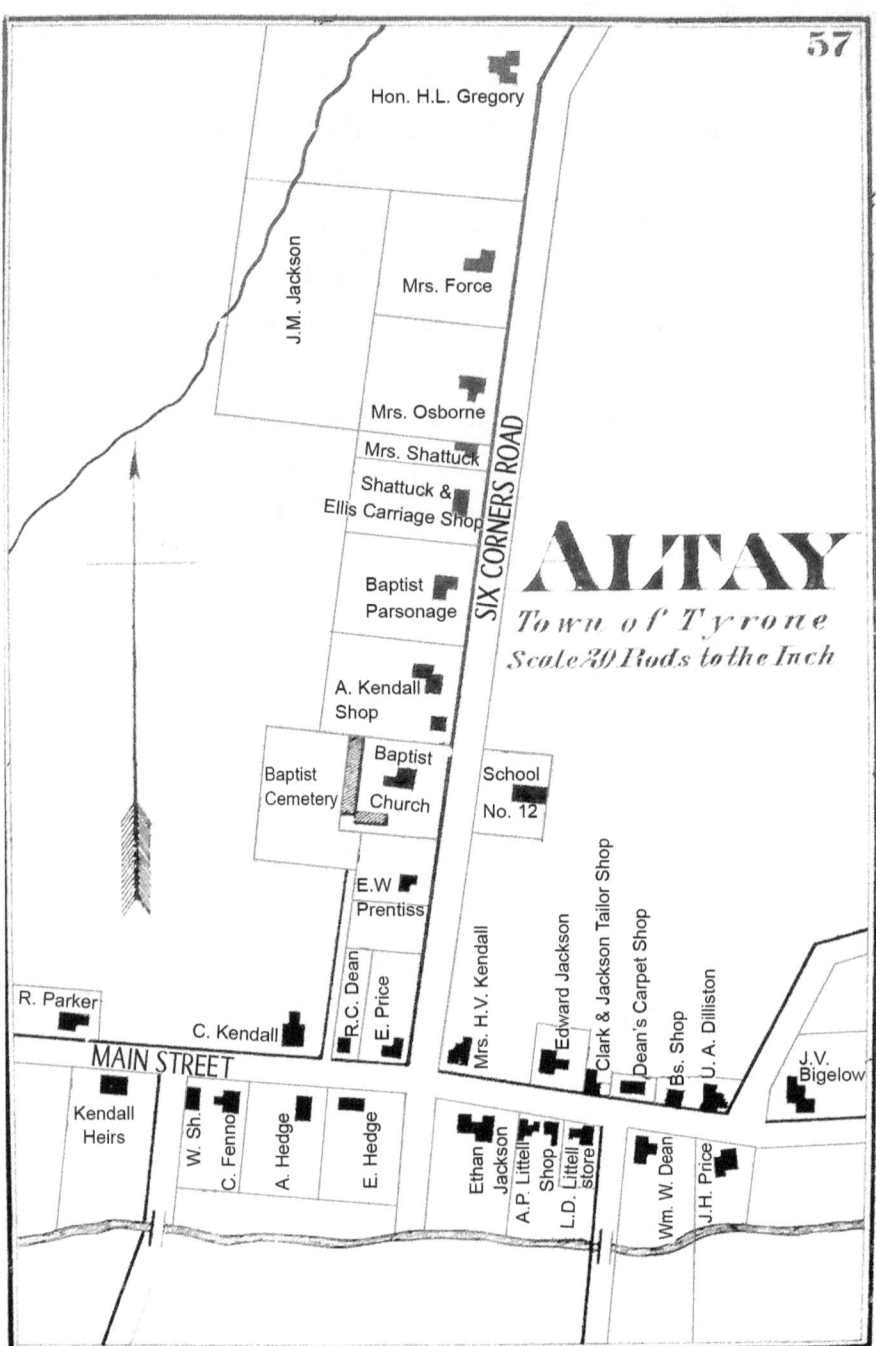

Altay is about twelve miles west of Watkins Glen, New York. Both maps are from *Atlas of Schuyler County, New York, 1874*. Above is a "cleaned up" version of the Altay map from the book. Although the maps are earlier than the diary, many of the homes and businesses that Viola mentioned are shown. The 1893-94 Schuyler County directory listed the Coolbaugh family's home on Main Street.

Home In These Hills

TYRONE

Scale 200 Rods to the Inch

People in this Diary

Viola's family in 1891

Pa - Major Coolbaugh, age 60, born in Yates County - assessor, clerk in post office and dealer in confectionary, tobacco and cigars
Ma - Susan Eaves Coolbaugh, age 52
Orville - brother, age 21, twin of Orson
Orson – brother, age 21, twin of Orville

Viola also had an older brother John who is not mentioned in diary.

Friends and Relations

Aunt Mate and Lola [Force] ages 32 and 3, lived in Tyrone, NY
Aunt Harriet [Kendall]
Aunt Dora
A. Eaves [Major A. Eaves] - a relative, lived in Weston, NY
Bert - friend of Orson
Homer Andrews
Elias [Bennett] - age 48, laborer
Jennie Bennett - age 20, lived in Tyrone
Mrs. Bigelow
Mr. [Eugene] Bigelow - age 36, farmer - owner of Tobyhanna Stock Farm
Alfred
Mr. & Mrs. Bonney
Mr. Brown
Katie Brown
Jennie Caldwell
Levanchie [Vanchie] Castner - age 27
Mr. Capman/Chapman - age 65, father of Flora
Flora [Chapman] - age 25
Mr. & Mrs. Castner [Isaac, age 51, wagonmaker & Sarah, age 51]
Charley & Tina
Leon Clark
Mrs. Cole
Aunt Fanny Coolbaugh - age 52, married to Squire
Uncle Squire Coolbaugh - age 62
Mrs. [Catherine] Corey - age 71
Mrs. [Nancy] Dean - age 62

Anna Dean – age 24
Susie Dillister/Dilliston - age 27
Mr. [Israel] Dillister - farmer
Edd & Nellie
Elbert
Alice Fenno
Charley Fenno
Mrs. Fenno - owned the Altay store
Mina Fenno - age 20
Satie [Sarah Fenno] - age 24
Uncle Frank Force - married to Mate [Mary]
Lola Force - age 3, daughter of Mate and Frank
Frank and Callie
Fred
Mr. & Mrs. Gasper [John - age 61, farmer and wife Hannah]
Georgie
Mrs. Gibbs
John/Johnnie Gregory - age 44, farmer in Altay - owned a shingle mill
Hamlin
Hattie
Dr. Harvey
Henry
Mrs. Hoff
Mr. Howell
Hannibal [Howell] - age 41, lived in Hornby
J. E. Hunt - age 47, shinglemaker
Mr. [Daniel] Jansen - farmer in Altay
Mrs. Rosetta Jansen
Jessie & Allie & Lillie & George
John & Rose & Emma
Mr. Johnson
Trude – Gertrude Kendall
George Kendall
Edna Kendall
Fred Kendall - owned 6 acres of raspberries
Erva Kendall
Mr. Lafever
Mr. [Henry] Lamb - age 36, farmer in Altay, also owned a saw mill and a basket factory

Amos Littell - age 67, farmer in Tyrone
Anna Littell - age 30
Ansyl/Ansel Littell - postmaster and farmer in Tyrone
Edith Littell - age 19 - school teacher
Ethan Littell - age 16 - farm laborer
Eunice Littell, age 39, mother of Edith and Ethan
Eugene Littell
Mr. Lockwood - age 48, farmer and beekeeper
Charley Losey - age 31, farmer in Tyrone - had an orchard
Emma Losey - age 30, married to Charley
Henry Losey - age 55, lived in Starkey
Mr. Maple [Mapes?]
Alice Mead - age 51, sister of Frank?
Frank Mead - age 45, farmer
Minnie – friend of Orville's
Aunt Mary McClure – age 77, lived in Altay
Dr. [George] Mottram - age 39, doctor, lived in Tyrone
Nellie
Mettie Osborn - age 44, dressmaker in Altay
Mr. Overton
Mrs. Palmer
Mrs. [Susanah] Parks - age 63, lived in Orange
Lessie [Celestia] Parks – age 29, lived in Orange
Amelia Parker
Eli Parker - age 31
Thannie People
Mr. Peck
Mr. Phelps
Mr. & Mrs. Pratt
Allen Price - age 30
Harvey Price
Jennie Rogers
Rose
Satie
Mrs. Sebring
Mr. Shannon
Aunt Isabelle Spicer – lived nearby
Uncle Charley Spicer
Stella & Ella
Susie

Mr. & Mrs. Swarthout
Mrs. Teller
Mrs. [Elizabeth] Tennant - age 32
Tina
Mr. & Mrs. Todd
William Townley
Mrs. Vangorder
Leora Walter
Mary Weller - age 51, lived on East Erie Avenue in Corning
Mr. & Mrs. Willover
Matie [Mary] Willover, age 22
Mr. [Arthur] Wintermute - owned the Altay Cheese factory
Mrs. [Nellie] Wixon
Mr. Worden
Elder Worth
Mr. & Mrs. Young/Yonge

The Altay school on Six Corners Road.

| Ther. | SAT. JAN. 3, 1891 | Wea. |

Cold. North wind. got up
at Six. did up the work
aired beds and pis—
Lurie McWhirter came here
we went up to Aunt
M's and Mr Byers
calling. Jennie Rogers
came down this evening
After she went home
Lurie & I went over to Mrs
Lewis.

| Ther. | SUNDAY 4 | Wea. |

Cold but pleasant wind
in the north east. went
to church and Sabbath
school this forenoon went
up to Auntie's after church
Mr J— came after Lurie
she went home with him
E— was here this evening
we were up to Auntie's a
little while.

Viola Coolbaugh
Altay, New York

Thursday, January 1, 1891

Warm, wind in the S, thawed, went up to Mr. Dillister's with Mr. J's folks. Alice Fenno called here this morning. Alfred & Mr. J[ansen?], Uncle Frank's folks spent the P.M. with Ma. Ma and I went over to Mrs. Dean's this evening. Anna L called here.

Friday, January 2, 1891

Warm, South wind some rain, evening growing colder, snow. Mr. & Mrs. Todd called here. I went up to Auntie's a few minutes. Satie [Sarah Fenno] and Mina [Fenno] & Alice spent the P.M. and evening with me. Knit one wristlet this P.M. Got up this morning at seven.

Saturday, January 3, 1891

Cold. North wind. Got up at six. Did up the work. Baked bread and pies. Susie Dillister came down this Evening. We went up to Aunt Mate's and Mr. Brown's calling. Jennie Rogers came down this Evening. After she went home. Susie & I went over to Mrs. Dean's.

Sunday, January 4, 1891

Cold but pleasant – wind in the northeast. Went to church and Sabbath school this forenoon. Went up to Auntie's after church. Mr. J came after Susie. She went home with him. S was here this evening. We were up to Auntie's a little while.

Monday, January 5, 1891

Cold. Wind in the East – got up at five – washed this forenoon and went over to Mrs. Dean's. Orson went to Corning. I went up to Mrs. Bigelow's and got some Butter. I went up to Jennie Rogers' and staid all night. Anna L[ittell] & Mrs. Fenno were here calling. Ida Ainsley died this Eve at five.

Tuesday, January 6, 1891
Cold but very pleasant. Wind in the East. Came home this morning - made a cake and helped do up the work. Mrs. Fenno & the two Mrs. Wixon's & Nellie, Auntie Mate and Lola were here visiting. I went over to Mr. Maple's this evening with Mr. Johnson.

Wednesday, January 7, 1891
Cold wind in the N.West. Got up at six. Georgie and I did up the work. Mrs. Sebring and Mrs. Hamlin and Mrs. Hoff were to Mr. Maple's to help. Mr. and Mrs. Pratt staid all night. Mr. Green was up to see about the Casket. Went to bed at ten.

Thursday, January 8, 1891
A lovely winter day - wind in the west. Got up at five. Georgie and I did up the work. They met at the house at eleven & left at twelve. Mrs. Palmer and I staid at the house and got dinner. Georgie and I took Mrs. P home. Went to bed at ten.

Friday, January 9, 1891
Cold, frosty morning. Wind in the north. Georgie and I did up the work. Mrs. M gave me a new white dress. Georgie brought me home this afternoon. We called to Trude's & Mrs. Tennant's. Went up to Mr. Shannon's to a surprise party.

Saturday, January 10, 1891
Cold this morning but getting warmer. Wind in the Southeast. Got home at 3:30 this morning. Did not get up until Eight. Went to R[ock] Stream this P.M. with Mr. J. Ma went up to Auntie's. Jennie Rogers was here this Evening.

Sunday, January 11, 1891
Rainy day. Wind in the south. Went to meeting this forenoon. Went over to Mrs. Dean's this afternoon. Did up her dinner work. It rained so I did not go to meeting this evening. Got up this morning at seven and went to bed at half past seven.

Postcard of Corning Glass Works factory, Corning, New York circa 1909. Publisher: The Rotograph Company, New York City.

Monday, January 12, 1891
Cold wind in the north and snow blowing terrible. Orville and Orson went to Corning to work in the glass factory. I helped Mrs. Bigelow today. She had company this evening. Mr. B and I went. There were thirty there. Got home at twelve.

Tuesday, January 13, 1891
Cold wind in the Northeast. Hung out our clothes this morning. Ma went up to Auntie's. I tended [the] Grocery most of the P.M. Called on Mrs. Dean a few minutes. Ma went over there this evening. I went up to Trude's. We played Parcheesi.

Wednesday, January 14, 1891
Getting warmer, wind in the West. Ironed this morning. Elbert came down and I went home with him. Allen Price's folks, Mr. Howell and Sister, Henry Losey's folks and Hattie, Elbert, Susie, and I went up to John Price's to a surprise party. Got home at half past one.

Viola attended the Altay Baptist Church. The church still exists on Six Corners Road.

Thursday, January 15, 1891
Not very warm, but wind in the southeast. Susie, Hattie and I went over to Mr. Lockwood's and spent the day. I learned how to Crochet some trimming. Susie and I went over to Allen Price's a little while. Went to bed at Eight.

Friday, January 16, 1891
A very pleasant day. Wind in the North. Got up at Eight. Elbert & Hattie came down to Mr. [Daniel] Jansen's and I came home. Finished my nightdress and went over to Mrs. Dean's calling. Went to Dundee to the Cantata with Mr. & Mrs. Jansen. Got home at eleven.

Saturday, January 17, 1891
Warmer wind in the South. Got up at six. Did up our Saturday's work. Mr. & Mrs. Jansen and Mr. Willover's family were here and spent the day. Auntie and Lola came down. Orville came home sick tonight. Ma and I called down to Mr. Fenno's this evening. Went to bed at ten.

Sunday, January 18, 1891
Cold and blustery. Wind in the north. Went to meeting and Sunday school. Elder Worth preached after dinner. Went over to Wm. Kendall's. Lo [Lola] and I went up to Nellie's this evening. Got home at nine. I went over to Mrs. Dean's this morning. Wrote to Orson.

Monday, January 19, 1891
Mild. Thawed some about noon. Wind in the south. Washed this forenoon. After dinner I went up to Auntie's and spent the afternoon. Ma and I called to Mrs. Dean's this evening. Anna Littell called here a few minutes.

Tuesday, January 20, 1891
Mild. Snow going quite fast. I went up to Eugene Bigelow's and staid with the girls while they went to Louis's funeral. Went up to Auntie's after dinner. Mrs. Gibbs's family were there. Ma went home with them. I ironed this evening. D. E. called here a few minutes.

Wednesday, January 21, 1891
Mild. A lovely day. Got up at six. Did up the work and finished ironing. Helped Pa clean the Grocery and cleaned out the hall this forenoon. Went up to Auntie's a little while this afternoon. Went down to John's to a surprise party. Started a little after five and got there at nine.

Thursday, January 22, 1891
Rainy. Arrived home at six o'clock this morning all safe but not very sound. Did not go to bed until night. Anna was over here a little while. E----- and D------- called here a few minutes. It is growing colder this afternoon. Good night.

Friday, January 23, 1891
Pleasant but colder – wind in the west. Got up at six. Did up the work and made a batch of Ginger Cookies and called down to Mr. Fenno's this forenoon. This afternoon Mina and I went up to Auntie's and called in to see Mrs. Brown. She is quite sick. Went to bed at ten.

Saturday, January 24, 1891
Pleasant and thawing. Wind in the south. Got up at six. Did up the work. Baked bread and pies and a Marble Cake. Went up to Auntie's a little while this afternoon. Orson came home. Mina was up and spent the evening with me. Alice Mead called here.

Sunday, January 25, 1891
Cold, but pleasant. Wind in the Northeast. Got up at seven did up the work and went to meeting and Sunday School. Uncle Squire and Aunt Fanny were here. I called up to Auntie's. Went to church this evening. Took a ride after church.

Monday, January 26, 1891
Cold, but growing warmer. Wind in the southeast. Got up at five. Did up the work and washed this forenoon. Orson went to Corning this morning. Churned and went a-calling this P.M. Auntie was here a few minutes. Ironed this evening.

New Year's Marble Cake

White part

whites of four eggs
one cup of sugar
half cup butter
half cup sweet milk
two teaspoons baking powder
one teaspoon vanilla or lemon [extract]
two and a half cups of sifted flour

Dark part

yolks of four eggs
one cup brown sugar
half cup molasses
half cup butter
half cup sour milk
one teaspoon cloves
one teaspoon cinnamon
one teaspoon mace
one teaspoon nutmeg
one teaspoon soda
one and a half cups sifted flour

Put it in the cake dish alternately, first one part and then the other.

| Ther. | TUES. JAN. 27, 1891 | Wea. |

Warm wind in the
south snow going fast
finished ironing and
straitened up the cup-
board and pantry Mr
Cooper was here to
dinner after dinner
I went up to Aunties
a little while Mina
called here this Evening

| Ther. | WEDNESDAY 28 | Wea. |

Warm and still thawing
wind in the South East
Ina came home to-day
Mr Gibbs family bright-
ley I called up to Mr
Browns and over to Mrs
Deans Mrs Jansen and
Myra Little called
here this Evening went
to bed at nine

Tuesday, January 27, 1891
Warm wind in the south. Snow going fast. Finished ironing and straitened up the cupboard and pantry. Mr. Gasper was here to dinner. After dinner I went up to Auntie's a little while. Mina called here this evening.

Wednesday, January 28, 1891
Warm and still thawing. Wind in the southeast. Ma came home today. Mr. Gibbs's family brought her. I called up to Mr. Brown's and over to Mrs. Dean's. Mrs. Jansen and Anna Littell called here this evening. Went to bed at nine.

Thursday, January 29, 1891
Warm and pleasant. Wind in the south. Corned down our beef this morning. Ma went up to Uncle Frank's. I called down to Mr. Fenno and over to Mrs. Dean's. Pa and George Kendall went to Tyrone. Mina and I went over to Prayer meeting. Had a terrible thundershower this evening.

Friday, January 30, 1891
Warm, but growing colder. Wind in the west. Went up and helped Auntie until three. Came home and got ready and up home with Frank Mead. I had a sleigh ride in mud. Went to bed at ten.

Saturday, January 31, 1891
Colder this morning but growing warmer. Wind in the southwest. Frank went over to Tyrone and got some cloth and I made Callie a cap. Had hickory nuts this afternoon. Went to bed at ten.

Sunday, February 1, 1891
Warmer. Looked very rainy but did not rain. Got up at seven. After dinner Frank brought Callie and I down home. Came in a wagon. Went over to Mrs. Dean's and down to Mr. Fenno's. Mina and I went to meeting this evening.

Monday, February 2, 1891
Colder. Wind in the northeast. Washed and cleaned up this forenoon. After dinner called to Mrs. Brown's and went up to Auntie's to stay this

week. Leora Walter's and [her] husband came and had to come home. Mina came up and spent the evening. Anna Littell had a little boy.

Tuesday, February 3, 1891
Warmer this morning but growing colder at noon. Tonight it is down to zero. Ma went up and staid with Auntie Dora and I went down to Mr. Fenno's and spent the afternoon. Anna's boy died this morning. Anna is very low.

Wednesday, February 4, 1891
Cold and blustery. Wind in the northwest. Ironed this forenoon. Dora went home this morning. Mina was up a few minutes. I went over to Trude's and Mrs. Dean's and down to Mr. Fenno's. I went up to Auntie's tonight to stay the rest of the week.

Thursday, February 5, 1891
Cold and windy. Wind in the southwest. Washed this morning. After dinner went down to school and over home a few minutes. Went to prayer meeting this evening and up to Mr. Gilbert's to a surprise party. Had a lovely time.

Friday, February 6, 1891
Warmer. Wind in the south. Thawing some. Ironed this forenoon and not do much of anything. This afternoon went down home. This evening called in to Mrs. Dean's and Mrs. Brown's. Went to the Temperance Lecture tonight.

Saturday, February 7, 1891
Warm wind in the south and thawing. Baked bread, and pies, and ginger cookies and a marble cake and cleaned up this forenoon. It snowed this afternoon and evening. Snow was about four inches deep at nine o'clock.

Sunday, February 8, 1891
Warm and pleasant. Thawing some snow about 8 inches deep this morning. Came home this morning. Auntie and Uncle and Lola came down. Aunty and I went to meeting. I went to church this evening. Took a sleigh ride after church. E--- was here

Auntie's Ginger Snaps

1 cup of molasses
½ cup butter
1 teaspoon soda
1 tablespoon ginger
enough flour to form a stiff dough

Mix ingredients. Roll as thin as possible. Bake in a moderate oven.

Monday, February 9, 1891
Blustery but not very cold. Wind in the south. Washed this forenoon and cleaned up after dinner. Wrote to Katie Brown and went down to Mr. Fenno's and over to Mrs. Dean's a few minutes. Went to bed at eight.

Tuesday, February 10, 1891
Squally and windy day. Wind in the north. I went over to Mrs. Dean's to help them. Ma was sick and I had to come home. Mrs. Wixon and Emma Losey and Anna Littell were here calling. Pa went over to Tyrone to town meeting. Went to bed at nine.

Wednesday, February 11, 1891
Cold but pleasant wind in the west. Thawed some this afternoon. Hung up the clothes and ironed the colored ones this afternoon. Ma is not feeling any better today. [She] Did not set [sit] up any. Aunty called here a few minutes.

Thursday, February 12, 1891
Cold this morning but thawing at noon. Snow is going fast. Ironed this forenoon and called over to Mrs. Dean's. Ma is feeling better. Went up

to Auntie's a few minutes this P.M. Mrs. Littell and Levanchie and Mrs. Fenno & Elder Worth were here.

Friday, February 13, 1891
Cold north wind this forenoon but growing warmer. Thawed some this afternoon. Pa went to Tyrone to mill. I went down and got me a pair of shoes. Came home with Uncle. Aunty and Lola were here this P.M. Ma is feeling better.

Saturday, February 14, 1891
Warmer wind in the south. Thawing some. Baked bread and pies and cake and cleaned up this forenoon. Orson came home this afternoon. I went down to Mr. Fenno's and over to Mrs. Dean's a few minutes. Mina was up this evening.

Sunday, February 15, 1891
Cold. South wind. Did not thaw much today. Pa and I went down to Uncle Squire's – found Aunt Fanny very low with typhoid pneumonia. Ma and the boys went up to Aunt Mate's. Went to church this evening. E--- and I went and took Erva [Kendall] home.

Monday, February 16, 1891
Warm and thawing this morning. Raining this afternoon. Washed and cleaned up this forenoon. Went over to Mrs. Dean's and down to John Gregory's and Frank Kendall's this afternoon. Satie Fenno and Anna L—[Littell] and Jim Bailey called here.

Tuesday, February 17, 1891
Warm and raining. Creek's quite high. Made a batch of ginger cookies. Went over to Mrs. Dean's. Anna [Dean] was so bad I staid all day. Mrs. Jansen was down. Anna died tonight at twenty minutes past ten.

Wednesday, February 18, 1891
A little colder and terrible windy. Mina [Fenno] was up this morning. Went over to Mrs. Dean's. Was there nearly all day and helped them. Mrs. Jansen came home with me to dinner. Orville came home from John's. Matie Willover was married.

Thursday, February 19, 1891
Cold but very pleasant. Wind in the southwest. Helped do up the work to home then went over to Mrs. Dean's and helped them bake. Aunty and Lola came down and spent the afternoon. Stella and Ella called here. Sara was up this evening.

Friday, February 20, 1891
A blustery sleety forenoon. Went over to Mrs. Dean's and helped do up the work. Went to Anna's funeral this forenoon. Nellie came home with me. Went to Sunday School Association this P.M. and evening. Mr. & Mrs. Bonney were here to tea.

Saturday, February 21, 1891
Warm and rainy. Did up the work and went over to Mrs. Dean's and Frank Kendall's. Orville went to Dundee with Frank to drive sheep. Uncle Frank was in here a few minutes. Anna Littell was here this evening. Pa was taken sick.

Sunday, February 22, 1891
Colder. Wind in the south. Went to meeting this morning. Come home and went to bed until dinner. Ate my dinner and went over to Mr. Phelp's and Mr. Capman's with Mr. Jansen's folks. Went to meeting this evening.

Monday, February 23, 1891
Cold and windy. Wind in the south. Washed this forenoon and cleaned up after dinner. Went over to Mrs. Dean's and Trude's and up to Aunt Mate's. Orville went down to Uncle Squires after Emma got home about six. Lola is quite sick.

Tuesday, February 24, 1891
Warmer. Wind in the south. Thawing some. Ironed this morning. Ma went up to Aunt Mate's and stayed with her. Lola is no better. Emma and I went up there this afternoon. I called over to Mrs. Dean's. She was not feeling as well.

| Ther. | SAT. FEB. 28, 1891 | Wea. |

It is still very cold and blustry wind in the north west — Emma and I did up the work baked Bread and pies Aunt is not feeling quite as well today set up to have her bed made. Good by February.

| Ther. | SUNDAY, MAR. 1 | Wea. |

A very cold day wind in the north Aunt is better Uncle went to Dundee after Mr Page Emma went down to Thau's Uncle Frank came after one I came home after dinner, went up to Annie's and to meeting This evening E— was here a little while

Wednesday, February 25, 1891
Stormy day. Wind in the south. Ma went up to Aunt Mate's and stayed with her. Lola is feeling a little better. Uncle was down here a few minutes. Satie was up here this afternoon. Emma and I wrote to Orson tonight.

Thursday, February 26, 1891
Colder. Snowing some. Wind in the north. I called up to Auntie's a little while. Lola is no better. Orville brought Emma and I down to Uncle Squire's. Aunt is better. The roads were terrible. Mr. & Mrs. Swarthout were up here this evening.

Friday, February 27, 1891
Cold and stormy. Wind in the north. Mrs. Vangorder went home this morning. Uncle took her. Emma and I did up the work and ironed. Aunt is feeling better but did not set up – only to have her bed made.

Saturday, February 28, 1891
It is still very cold and blustery. Wind in the northwest. Emma and I did up the work. Baked bread and pies. Aunt is not feeling quite as well today. Set up to have here bed made. Goodbye February.

Sunday, March 1, 1891
A very cold day. Wind in the north. Aunt is better. Uncle went to Dundee after Mr. Page. Emma went down to Frank's. Uncle Frank came after me. I came home after dinner. Went up to Auntie's and to meeting this evening. L--- was here a little while.

Monday, March 2, 1891
A stinging cold morning. Wind in the north. Went up to Auntie's and washed this forenoon. After dinner went up to the store and got me a pair of rubbers. Went over to Mrs. Dean's. Mrs. Castner was over here. Cut out my pantalets.

Tuesday, March 3, 1891
Cold and blustery. Wind in the South. Helped do up the morning work and washed this forenoon. Pa and Orville drew hay this af-

ternoon. I went up to Eugene Bigelow's. Anna Littell was here a little while. Ma went over to Mrs. Castner's.

Wednesday, March 4, 1891
A blustery, stormy, windy day. Wind in the south. I went up to Auntie's and ironed this forenoon. Called into Mr. Brown's on my way home. Went over to Mrs. Dean's and Mrs. Castner's. Called down to Mr. Fenno's this evening.

Thursday, March 5, 1891
Cold and blustery in the forenoon. Quite pleasant this afternoon. Mrs. Fenno and Mrs. Jansen and Anna Littell were here calling. Ma went up to Auntie's. Mina and I went to prayer meeting. I made my pantalets.

Friday, March 6, 1891
A cold, but pleasant day. Wind in the north did up the morning work and went down to Mina's and got her valise and went to Dundee to go to Hornby [Dundee to Hornby is about 28 miles] with Emma. She was not going until Tuesday so I came home. Anna L was here this evening.

Saturday, March 7, 1891
Cold but somewhat pleasant. Wind in the west. Orville went to the depot after some things after dinner. I went down to John Gregory's. Called into Mrs. Dean's a few minutes. Anna L was here a few minutes.

Sunday, March 8, 1891
Warm wind in the south. Looked very much like rain but did not rain any. Went to meeting and Sunday School. Went up to Uncle's to dinner. Called to Stella's and Mr. Brown's. Went to meeting this evening. I went home with Auntie.

Monday, March 9, 1891
A very rainy day. It rained so we did not wash. Made Pa a pair of pants. I went over to Mrs. Dean's a few minutes and up to the store and got

Brown Bread

Two cups of Indian meal even full, three cups of flour or Graham meal heaped, a pint and a half of sour milk, a cup of molasses, teaspoonful and a half of soda, one of saltm steamed for four hours. Brown lightly in the oven afterwards.

A postcard view of the Dundee, New York depot of the Northern Central Railroad (Lyons Branch). This was the closest station to Altay - about 7½ miles.

some thread. Called over to Mrs. Castner's. Anna Littell was over a few minutes this evening.

Tuesday, March 10, 1891
Colder this morning but growing warmer. Wind in the south. We washed this forenoon and cleaned up. Fixed over my nightdress this afternoon. Called to Mrs. Tennant's. Auntie was down a little while. Went down to Mr. Fenno's this evening.

Wednesday, March 11, 1891
A lovely day. Wind in the south. I ironed this morning. Ma and Pa cleaned the Grocery. Anna came over and got some milk. Mrs. Teller moved today. I went over to Anna's and spent the afternoon. Orville went to Dundee.

Thursday, March 12, 1891
A very rainy day but warm wind in the south. Cleaned pantry this forenoon. Ma went over to Mrs. Castner's visiting this afternoon. Aunt Mate came down. We went to the store and called to Mrs. C. Mina was up this evening.

Friday, March 13, 1891
A very windy day. Rainy this forenoon. Wind in the west. Ma went up to Aunt Mate's. I commenced some trimming for Aunt Fanny. Ma and I called up to Mrs. Tennant's and Mrs. Teller's this evening.

Saturday, March 14, 1891
Wind blowing. A Jimy[?] came. We baked bread, cake and pies and cleaned up this forenoon. Called into Mrs. Dean's this afternoon. Auntie came down and we went to the store. Orson came home this afternoon. Went to bed at eight.

Sunday, March 15, 1891
Some warmer. Wind in the south. Went to meeting and Sunday school after dinner. Went over to Frank Kendall's. Mina came up this evening and we went to Endeavor Meeting. Did not stay to church. Went up to N.L. after meeting.

Monday, March 16, 1891
Cold and windy. We washed this morning but did not hang up the clothes. Orville and Pa worked in the woods this afternoon. I tended the P.O. Ma called over to Mrs. Dean's. Sent for the Sabbath School Quarterlies.

Tuesday, March 17, 1891
Cold but very pleasant and still. Hung out our clothes this morning. I tended [the] Grocery. Pa and Orville worked in the woods. I called to Mrs. Tennant's and Mrs. Teller's this evening. Ma and I went up to Aunt Mate's a few minutes.

Wednesday, March 18, 1891
Warmer wind in the south. Ironed a little this morning and Ma finished. I went up to Mr. Bigelow's and staid with the children while they went to Reading [New York]. Called into Tina's on my way home. Went over to Mrs. Dean's this evening.

Thursday, March 19, 1891
Warm and pleasant wind in the south. Pa drawed wood. Orville went to Allen Price's. I went over to Trude's and made her a batch of sugar and ginger cookies. Aunt was down. Eugene Littell was hurt very bad. Mina and I went to Prayer Meeting.

Friday, March 20, 1891
A very rainy day. Wind in the south. Did not do much of anything today. Went up to Eugene Bigelow's and got some butter. Called into Mrs. Teller's. Orville and I went over to David's to a surprise party. There were only a few there.

Saturday, March 21, 1891
A foggy and unpleasant day. Got home this morning at three. Did not get up until six. Ma made bread and ginger cookies and pies. Ma went up to Auntie's and spent the afternoon. I went up and came home with her. Anna L, Jennie C, & Nellie B were here.

A postcard view of Market Street in Corning, New York, circa 1905. Publisher unknown.

Lemon Pie

One cup of hot water
one tablespoon of corn-starch
one cup of white sugar
one tablespoon of butter
juice and grated rind of one lemon

Cook for a few minutes; add one egg; bake with a top and bottom crust.

Rhubarb Pie

Skin the stalks, cut in small pieces; line the plate and cover well with the raw fruit; strew lavishly with sugar, and sprinkle over this a little flour. Cover and bake about three-quarters of an hour. This, like all fruit pies is eaten cold.

Sunday, March 22, 1891
A very dull day. Went to meeting this morning. Had the toothache and did not stay to Sunday School. After dinner I went up to Auntie's and called to Mettie Osborn's. Went up to church this evening. It rained quite hard when I came home.

Monday, March 23, 1891
A very rainy day. We washed but did not hang out our clothes. Made a silver cake this morning and commenced some edging for a skirt. Had that toothache. Edna and Jennie were here calling this evening.

Tuesday, March 24, 1891
Warm but looked so stormy we did not hang up our clothes. I called into Mr. Fenno's and Frank Kendall's and Mrs. Dean's this forenoon. After dinner I went up to Mr. Jansen's and staid all night called into Auntie's.

Wednesday, March 25, 1891
A lovely day. I came home this morning after nine. Ma hung out the clothes. Jessie & wife & Allie & Lillie & George were here and spent the day. I went up to Eugene L--- a-calling after they went home.

Thursday, March 26, 1891
Another lovely day. Wind in the north. Ironed this forenoon. Mina was up calling. I went to the depot with Mr. Castner. Came to Corning. Jennie met me at the depot. Orson and Bert came up to Jennie's this evening.

Friday, March 27, 1891
A cloudy and unpleasant day. Helped Jennie do up her work and then crocheted some this forenoon. Rote a letter home this morning. Went down to Mary Weller's a-calling. Fred went uptown this evening.

Saturday, March 28, 1891
A lovely day. Jennie and I did up the morning work and then I crocheted a little. After dinner, Orson came up and I went up to Hornby on the stage. Called to Hannibal's and Amos's and Henry's. Staid all night to Uncle Charley's.

Sunday, March 29, 1891
Another lovely day. Wind in the north. Went to Sunday School and Meeting. This forenoon went to Amos's and up to Henry's. After dinner I wrote two letters. Emma and I went over to Endeavor Meeting this evening.

Monday, March 30, 1891
Another very fine day. Aunt Isabelle and I washed this morning. Henry and Orson went to Corning. Emma and I went to school. After dinner I went up to Hannibal's and spent the afternoon. The young people met here tonight.

Tuesday, March 31, 1891
It snowed nearly all day. I helped Aunt iron and then went up to Henry's a few minutes. After dinner went down to Amos's and spent the afternoon and evening. Aunt and Emma came down this evening.

Wednesday, April 1, 1891
Pleasant but muddy. I went up to Henry's and staid all day. Emma went to School. Addie came up to the Henry's this afternoon. Emma and I went to the Minstrel show this evening. Got home at half-past ten.

Thursday, April 2, 1891
A very stormy day. It rained this forenoon and snowed this afternoon. Aunt Isabelle & Uncle Charley and I went up to Hannibal's and spent the day. Had a lovely time. Made maple sugar and wax and had a good time in general.

Friday, April 3, 1891
A nasty muddy day. Snow thawing off. Went down to Amos's this forenoon. Aunt Charley and Aunt Isabelle came down to dinner. Went up to Henry's this afternoon. This evening Emma and I went to the show to the Town Hall.

Saturday, April 4, 1891
A cold windy day. Came down to Jennie's this forenoon. Got there about twelve. Orson came up and brought me my valise. Jennie and I went downtown this afternoon. Fred went this evening.

Sunday, April 5, 1891
A cold windy day but quite bright. Fred, Jennie and I went to church this morning. Called to Mrs. Parks on my way home. Orson and Bert came up here this afternoon. Did [not] feel very well this afternoon. Wrote a letter home.

Monday, April 6, 1891
A lovely day. Jennie washed this forenoon. I did not do much of anything. Did not feel very well. Got dinner and then laid down the rest of the day. Jennie sewed on her dress. Fred went uptown this evening.

Tuesday, April 7, 1891
A very windy day but still quite pleasant. Did not feel very well. Lounged around all of the forenoon and after dinner Jennie and I went down town. Got Ma a new dress. Orson and Bert were up this evening.

Wednesday, April 8, 1891
A lovely day. Helped Jennie do up her morning work and then went downtown. Went up in the glass factory. I came home today. Pa met me at the depot. Auntie and Lola were down. Ma and I called to Tina's.

Thursday, April 9, 1891
A very fine day. Helped do up the morning work and then tended the Post Office. Pa and Orville worked in the woods. Ma went up to Auntie's. This afternoon Satie and Mina called here. We went to Prayer Meeting.

Friday, April 10, 1891
A rainy day. Helped do up the morning's work. Ironed my clothes and went over to Aunt Harriet's [Kendall] and got some butter. Went up to the store and got a can of tomatoes. Called into Mrs. Teller's. Mina was up. Worked on Ma's dress.

Saturday, April 11, 1891
Another dull stormy day. Helped do up the morning's work. Went up to the store and got some buttons for Ma's dress. We finished it. Made me an apron. Went up to Auntie's this afternoon. Staid all night. Aunt and I called on Mettie.

| Ther. | WED. APRIL 15, 1891 | Wea. |

A very nice day ironed this forenoon finished got dinner did up the work and mended untill four then went up home a few minuets called into Johny Gregorys Pawtle to Parsons this afternoon.

| Ther. | THURSDAY 16 | Wea. |

Another lovely day did up the work and cleaned up and churned this forenoon after dinner I mended untill supper time then skimed milk and sponged bread and got supper

Pork Cake

half a pound of salt pork - chopped fine
two cups of molasses
half pound of raisins - chopped well
two eggs
two teaspoons each of clove, allspice and mace
half a tablespoon of saleratus or soda and flour enough to make a stiff batter

The oven must not be too hot.

Sunday, April 12, 1891
A cloudy day. Aunty and I got up at six. After breakfast went home and got ready for Meeting, After dinner called up to Mrs. Bigelow's. Mina came up and went to meeting this evening. L--.

Monday, April 13, 1891
A lovely day. Went down to Mr. Wintermute's this morning. Washed and cleaned up. Had a monstrous big wash. Did not get through until after three. Got supper. Did up the work and then went to bed.

Tuesday, April 14, 1891
Another lovely day. Got up at six. Got breakfast and did up the work and then went to ironing. Got dinner and did up the work and then ironed until suppertime. Mrs. Young went down to Mr. Kendall's. Rainy this evening.

Wednesday, April 15, 1891
A very nice day. Ironed this forenoon. Finished. Got dinner. Did up the work and mended until four. Went up home a few minutes. Called into Johnny Gregory's. I wrote to Orson this afternoon. A.D.U.

Thursday, April 16, 1891
Another lovely day. Did up the work and cleaned up and churned this forenoon. After dinner I mended until suppertime then skimmed milk and sponged bread and got supper.

Friday, April 17, 1891
A lovely day. Wind in the south. Baked bread and did up the forenoon's work. After dinner starched the clothes and hung them up and then went up home a few minutes.

Saturday, April 18, 1891
A very nice day. Did up the work. Baked pies, fried cakes – pork cake and white cake. Ironed and churned and cleaned up. Mrs. Young and Mr. Young and I went up to John Gregory's calling. Did not find them home.

Sunday, April 19, 1891
A very nice day. Helped Mrs. Young do up the work then went up home. Cut Pa's hair and got ready for meeting. After dinner Jennie and I went to the woods. Went up to Auntie's and to meeting.

Monday, April 20, 1891
A lovely day. Did not go down to Mr. Young's. My rist hurt so I could not work. Ma washed and cleaned up. I tended the Post Office. Went over to Aunt Harriet's and Mrs. Dean's. Had a present of a Bible through the mail.

Tuesday, April 21, 1891
A very fine day. I ironed this morning and helped do up the work. Went up and called on Aunty McClure [Mary] and Mrs. Dean. She gave me one of Anna's skirts. Came down to John's this afternoon.

Wednesday, April 22, 1891
A very nice day. Helped Rose do up her morning work and picked a mess of greens for dinner. Read *A Fatal Wedding Day*. Rose and I did not do much this afternoon.

Thursday, April 23, 1891
A very fine day. Looked like showers in the afternoon but did not get any. I finished reading *A Fatal Wedding Day* this evening. Rose and John and I went up to Mr. Allan's. I hired out to tie grape vines for 75 cents per day.

Friday, April 24, 1891
Colder this morning and looked quite stormy. Helped Rose do up the morning work. Minnie took me to the depot after dinner. Came to Dundee. Went up to Mr. Chapman's. Ma came down after. Emma and I got home at six.

Saturday, April 25, 1891
A splendid day. Did up the morning work. Baked bread, pies and cake. Ma went up to Auntie's and made her a batch of ginger cookies. Orville and Orson came home. We went to the Sugar Festival. Took in $10.60.

Sunday, April 26, 1891
A splendid day. Went to Meeting and Sunday School. After dinner went up to Auntie's a little while. Went over to Trude's and Harriet's. Ma and I went to church this evening. Had a splendid meeting. Collection $1.00.

Monday, April 27, 1891
A lovely day. I took Orville nearly to the depot. Orson and Bert went later – and went a-foot. Ma washed. I did not feel very well. Tended Post Office. Pa drawed out manure all day.

Tuesday, April 28, 1891
A very pleasant day. Ma ironed. I did not feel very well and did not do much of anything. Pa finished drawing out manure. Mina was up here a few minutes. Frank Kendall was also here calling.

Wednesday, April 29, 1891
Another pleasant day. Pa plowed our garden and commenced [plowing] Mr. Lamb's [garden]. Ma tended the Post Office and did the work. I am feeling better but did not do anything. Mina and Aunt Mate were here.

Thursday, April 30, 1891
A pleasant day but windy. Pa dragged the garden this forenoon and marked it out. This afternoon Aunt Mate and Mrs. Force and Lola were down and spent the afternoon. Theresa, Maud, and Bertha called.

Friday, May 1, 1891
A very pleasant day. Wind in the south. Jennie called here today [at] noon. Mrs. Teller came down and spent the afternoon. Auntie and Lola called here a few minutes this evening. Pa planted some of this garden.

Saturday, May 2, 1891
A cloudy day. Looked quite story but did not rain. Pa finished plowing Mr. Lamb's garden and drew a load of hay and made some more garden. Satie Fenno was here calling this afternoon.

Sunday, May 3, 1891
Rained a little this forenoon but cleared off and was very pleasant this afternoon. Charley & Tina and L.E. Kendall & Mettie Osborn & Jennie Caldwell & Mrs. Castner & Uncle Frank & Mr. Price called here. I wrote a letter to A. Eaves this P.M.

Monday, May 4, 1891
A windy and somewhat cold day. Ma washed this morning. I did up the housework and got dinner. Ma made bread this forenoon. She went up to Aunt's a few minutes this P.M. I ironed. Mina called here this evening.

Tuesday, May 5, 1891
A cold windy day. Ma cleaned one room up stairs. I did the work and finished ironing. Ma churned this morning. I went over to Mrs. Dean's a little while. Mrs. Fenno came up and spent the afternoon with us. Jennie called here.

Wednesday, May 6, 1891
A raw cold day. Ground covered with snow this morning. Ma finished cleaning upstairs. I made two pair of pillowcases and sewed the trimming on my skirt. Satie & Mina and I called up to Mrs. Bigelow's and Mrs. McClure's.

Thursday, May 7, 1891
Cold this morning but growing warmer. Ma and I went down to Uncle Squire's this morning. Got home at half-past four. Called into Frank Kendall's. Satie, Mina and I went to Prayer Meeting.

Friday, May 8, 1891
A pleasant day but windy. Helped do up the work then went up to Auntie's and called to Mettie's and Mr. Brown's. Satie and Mina and I went to school this afternoon. Mettie called here this evening.

Saturday, May 9, 1891
A very warm day. We did our Saturday's work and cleaning. Pa carried the potatoes out of the cellar. After, Pa went to Charley Fenno's vendue

Cherry Pie

Line the dish and fill up with ripe cherries, regulatating the quantity of sugar you use by their sweetness; sift over this a small teaspoonful of flour, add a very little butter, then cover and bake.

[auction]. Ma went up to Aunt Mate's a little while. Satie, Mina and I called to Mr. Yonge's and to John Gregory's this evening.

Sunday, May 10, 1891
A pleasant, but very warm day. Went to meeting and then went up home with Mr. and Mrs. Jansen. We went up to Charley Losey's and called. Went to meeting this evening. Did not get there to the Young Peoples' Meeting.

Monday, May 11, 1891
Not very pleasant – cold and windy this forenoon but growing warmer this afternoon. We washed and laid our white clothes out on the grass. Ma and I went to Tyrone and got some paper and Ma got her a new hat. Wrote to A.U. tonight.

Tuesday, May 12, 1891
A very nice day. Did up the work and tore up the Parlor. Eli Parker papered for us, we got our room cleaned and settled. Mrs. Fenno and Trude and Jennie and Aunty and Lola were here calling. Went over to Mrs. Dean's a-calling this evening.

Wednesday, May 13, 1891
Cold this morning but a lovely day. Helped do up the morning work and then went over to Trude's and helped clean. We cleaned six rooms. Ma cleaned her bedroom and clothes room. Aunt and Lola were here a little while.

Thursday, May 14, 1891
A pleasant day but cold north wind. Helped Trude clean house. We cleaned the dining room and bedroom. Called down to Mr. Fenno's. Mina and I went to prayer meeting. Orson came home. Cleaned the cellar.

Friday, May 15, 1891
Another nice day. We cleaned the hall. Orson and I papered and Ma cleaned and did the rest of the work. Auntie was down a few minutes this evening. Orson went to Rock Spring and I went over to Mr. Maple's this evening.

Saturday, May 16, 1891
A cold and windy day. Wind in the north. Moved our kitchen stove this morning and took up the carpet and cleaned up a little. Did our Sat[urday] work. Pa and I went to Tyrone this P.M. Carrie Harris died this evening.

Sunday, May 17, 1891
A windy day bit quite pleasant. Went to church and Sunday School. After dinner, Ma and I went up to Auntie's. I called to Mettie's, and we went to singing school and up to Mrs. McClure's and Mr. Bigelow's. Went to church this evening.

Monday, May 18, 1891
A very windy day. Ma washed but did not hang up the clothes. Pa took Orson to the Depot. He went to Corning. I cleaned the pantry this forenoon. Mettie and I went to the woods after moss. Mina and I went down to Mr. Wintermute's.

Tuesday, May 19, 1891
A lovely day. Hung up our clothes this morning and churned. Mina and Mettie and I decorated the church for Carrie Harris's funeral. Mrs. Shoemaker was here and took dinner. Auntie & Lola were down this evening. Mina & I went down to Mr. W---.

Wednesday, May 20, 1891
A windy dusty day but pleasant otherwise. Ironed this morning. Aunt brought Lola down to stay with us while she went to the Anniversary to Mr. Overton's. We called to Mrs. Dean's and Trude's. I went down to Amelia Parker's a few minutes this evening.

Thursday, May 21, 1891
A somewhat cold day. Looked stormy but did not rain to amount to anything. I cleaned Mrs. Dean's sitting room and bedroom. Ma patched our kitchen [wall]paper and made a feathertick. Satie and Mina and I went to prayer meeting.

Home of Frank, Gertrude, and Edna Kendall in Altay, NY.

Downtown Altay, New York today.

Hints for Making Cake

The flour should always be very dry and well sifted.
White sugar is purer and sweeter for cakes and pastries than brown sugar.
If the butter is very hard, soften, but do not melt it.
The butter and sugar should be worked into a cream.
Eggs should be broken separately in a cup, then if one is bad, it will not spoil the others; they should be cold to beat well; always use a shallow dish in whipping the whites; and never stop after you commence beating them until they are light; unless they are very fresh do not try to whip them until you can turn the dish over without their slipping.
When soda is used, dissolve it before adding to the general mixture.
Fruit should be thoroughly dry; as, if added to the other ingredients damp, cakes will liable to be heavy. Dust your fruit with a little flour to be used for the cake, and stir into the other ingredients just before putting in the rest of the flour. The ingredients should be well beaten before mixing in the flour, except in a few plain cakes that are beaten all together.
All cakes bake nicer if the pans used are lined with buttered paper.
To know when a cake is sufficiently baked, insert a knitting needle, or clean broom corn, draw it out, and if it does not look the least sticky the baking is finished.

Friday, May 22, 1891
Stormy this morning but did not rain much. Pa and I went and turned Flora out over to Homer Andrews. After dinner Satie and I went to Tyrone. Sate and Mina & Jennie & I went up to Mr. Peck's. Eugene B[igelow]'s team run away.

Saturday, May 23, 1891
A lovely day. Did up the morning work. Baked and cleaned up in general. Eli White [white]washed this afternoon. I went to church meeting. Callie came home with me. We called to Eugene L[ittell]. Orville and Minnie came up tonight.

Sunday, May 24, 1891
A pleasant day but cold wind. Went to church and Sunday School. Elder Worth came home with me. Uncle Squire and Aunt Fanny were up. Went to Singing School and to meeting this evening. Came home with the sick headache.

Monday, May 25, 1891
A very nice day. We washed this morning. Eli finished our whitewashing. Cleaned my bedroom and papered the sitting room. Called into Mrs. Dean's this forenoon. Frank and Mettie called here. Went to bed a little before nine.

Tuesday, May 26, 1891
A cloudy cold day but did not rain much. I finished the sitting room and called to Trude's and Mettie's and up to Mr. Peck's this forenoon. Went to Ella Phelps's funeral this P.M. Called to Mr. Brown's this evening. Went up to Auntie's.

Wednesday, May 27, 1891
A pleasant day. Had a hard frost this morning. Did up the work and ironed some. Ma finished cleaning the dining room. Ma went up to Auntie's this P.M. I ironed some. Ansill [Ansyl/Ansel], Mina, and Mrs. Wixon were here this evening.

Thursday, May 28, 1891
A lovely day. Finished ironing my dress and skirt. After dinner went

down to Mr. Fenno's and up to Aunt Mate's. Went to Prayer meeting. Went over to Trude's to Edna's birthday party.

Friday, May 29, 1891
A lovely day. Ethan [Littell] came over after me to help them with hay pressers. Eunice [Littell] and I baked and ironed after dinner. We went up after Edith [Littell]. Come home. Got supper. Did up the work and went to bed. It rained some tonight.

Saturday, May 30, 1891
A beautiful morning after the rain. Made pies and cleaned up this forenoon. Had an early dinner and Edith, Eunice and Ethan & I went to Dundee. Nellie came home with us. We went over to Eugene's this evening. Rooster crow[ed].

Sunday, May 31, 1891
A lovely day. Got up at seven. Did up the work and all went to meeting. I staid over home until after evening services. Met [Mettie] took Edith up home. Ma and I called to Auntie's. Met and I went to singing school this P.M. and called to Harvey Price's.

Monday, June 1, 1891
A fine day. Did up the morning work and baked bread. Eunie & Nellie washed. I helped a little and churned and cleaned up. We all took a nap this afternoon. Went down to Johnnie Gregory's this evening.

Tuesday, June 2, 1891
A pleasant day. Eunie and Ansyl went to the Depot with Eugene's folks. He went to Elmira [Elmira Water Cure] to be treated. I baked pies, ginger cookies and silver cake. Mrs. Simenson called here this evening. Had a fine shower.

Wednesday, June 3, 1891
A very warm day. Did up the morning work. Moped [mopped] and cleaned up some and baked bread. Eunie and I called to Mr. Worden's this afternoon. We all went over town this evening. The pressers broke down.

Silver Cake

Two cups of flour
One cup of butter
a cup of milk
one cup of sugar
yolks of three eggs
one teaspoonful of soda
two teaspoonfuls of cream of tartar

[There are no other instructions listed. Apparently good bakers knew what to do!]

Ther.   THURS. JUNE 4, 1891   Wea.

A pleasant but cool day we did up our work and ironed the pressers were here but did not press any got ready to commence Eunice & I called to Mrs Siminsons Eunice & Ethan & I came over with Ethan Mina & I went begging had good luck

Ther.   FRIDAY 5   Wea.

A heavy frost this morning we did our work & back and cleaned up this forenoon the hay pressers finished this afternoon after dinner we put down the carpet I came home Mina and I made ten quarts of Ice Cream

Thursday, June 4, 1891
A pleasant but cool day. We did up our work and ironed. The pressers were here but did not press any. Got ready to commence. Eunie & I came over town. Ethan, Mina & I went begging. Had good luck.

Friday, June 5, 1891
A heavy frost this morning. We did our work, baked, and cleaned up this forenoon. The hay pressers finished this forenoon. After dinner we put down the carpet. I came home. Mina and I made ten quarts of ice cream.

Saturday, June 6, 1891
A cloudy and cold day. Did the morning work and cleaned up and baked. Worked over to the church all the afternoon freezing ice cream. Went to the festival this evening. Had a fine time. Took in $14.25.

Sunday, June 7, 1891
A lovely day. Mina and I went and swept out the church and dusted. Went to meeting and Sunday School. Went up to Mr. Dillesten's with Mr. & Mrs. Jansen. We all came to church this evening.

Monday, June 8, 1891
A splendid day. We did up the morning work and washed and churned

Ice Cream

Take three pints of milk, four eggs, well beaten, three-fourths pound of sugar, and one tablespoonful of corn-starch; mix in a three-quart tin pail, boil in a kettle of water till quite thick; add one pint of sweet cream and flavor to taste. Freeze in a common water pail, or any vessel of suitable size, with equal parts of ice chopped fine, and coarse salt. Rotate the pail and stir frequently.

Viola Coolbaugh

this forenoon. After dinner Mina and I went and washed up the dishes. We went up to Mett's this evening. Aunt and Lola were here.

Tuesday, June 9, 1891
A lovely day but very dusty. Ironed this forenoon. Went to Tyrone this afternoon. Got me a new hat. Tina went with me. Orson worked for Mr. Jansen. Pa was worse today. Aunt and Lola were down a few minutes today.

Wednesday, June 10, 1891
A lovely day. Helped up the morning work. Went over and helped Trude clean. Pa is feeling better today. Orson helped Mr. Jansen this forenoon. Aunt and Lola were down a little while. Orson and I went to Tyrone this evening.

Thursday, June 11, 1891
A lovely day. Looked quite rainy but did not rain until night. Did up the morning work. Uncle brought Lola down. Carrie, Fred, and I went to Glenora to the Price and Force Reunion. Had a lovely time.

Friday, June 12, 1891
A lovely day. Did up the morning work and washed the windows and mopped upstairs this forenoon. After dinner, Mina, Mettie, Edna and Flora and I worked over to the church until suppertime.

Saturday, June 13, 1891
A terrible warm day. Did up the morning work. Ma washed my pansy dress. Worked over to the church all day. Mina and I went up on East Hill after flowers this afternoon. Fixed my white dress.

Sunday, June 14, 1891
A lovely day. Mina and I went over to church and watered the plants. Went to church and Sunday School this forenoon. Edna came home with me. Went to church - this evening [went to] concert. Mrs. & Mrs. Bonney called here.

Monday, June 15, 1891

A very warm day. Washed and did up the work this morning then went over to church and worked until noon. Mettie and I carried the plants home this evening. Lola went with us.

Tuesday, June 16, 1891

Another terrible warm day. Ironed this forenoon. Aunty and Lola came down. Had a terrible thunderstorm. Orville helped Fred Kendall this forenoon. Orson went to Watkins [Glen].

Wednesday, June 17, 1891

A nice day. Quite warm this forenoon but cooler this afternoon. Ironed my pansy dress this forenoon and went up to Mr. Brown's and got some lettuce. Aunt and I went up to Mrs. Bigelow's this afternoon. It rained some.

Thursday, June 18, 1891

A nasty rainy day. Made a batch of ginger cookies and a pie. Ma went down to Mrs. Fenno's this afternoon. Jennie Caldwell was here. Mrs. Bigelow, Mr. Lafever, and Mrs. Cole called here. I worked on my dress.

Friday, June 19, 1891

A cloudy day. Looked very rainy but did not rain. Ma and I finished cleaning the grocery this forenoon. Orson went after a load of coal for Mr. Lamb. Aunt and Lola were down a few minutes. Had a terrible toothache.

Saturday, June 20, 1891

A very nice day. Did up the Saturday's work and cleaning this forenoon. After dinner, Orson got some strawberries and then we took care of them. Aunt & Lola & Mrs. Dean called here. Went over to George Pierce's this evening.

Sunday, June 21, 1891

A rainy day. Helped do up the morning work and went to meeting and Sunday School. After church went up to Auntie's. Ma came up this afternoon. Went to meeting this evening. There was not many at it.

Custard Pie

Make a custard of a quart of milk, six eggs - well beaten, a cup of white sugar - not heaped, and a teaspoon of vanilla. Line your plates with paste, pour in the custard and bake immediately. If you wish pudding, line your plate with paste and bake thick.

Monday, June 22, 1891
A cloudy morning but cleared off. We washed and cleaned up this forenoon after dinner. Ma went over to Trude's to get her cape cut. Pa went up to Mr. Peck's and spent the afternoon. Aunt and Lola were here. Had a thundershower.

Tuesday, June 23, 1891
A lovely day. Mrs. Castner, Orville, Orson and I commenced to clean the church. Got the back room all cleaned. Aunt and Lola were down here this afternoon. Ma and I went down to Mr. Fenno's this evening.

Wednesday, June 24, 1891
Another very fine day. Orville and Orson and I cleaned [the] Church all day. Mrs. Caster helped this forenoon. Aunt and Lola and Mrs. Brown called on us. I went up to the store. Trude was over here.

Thursday, June 25, 1891
A terrible warm day. Orville, Orson, Mrs. Castner, and I finished cleaning the church. Orville and Orson went to Tyrone to a ballgame this P.M. Altay boys got beat. Aunt and I went strawberrying. I went to prayer meeting.

Friday, June 26, 1891
A very warm day. Went over to Trude's. She and Edna went up to Warsaw [NY - not the one in Wyoming County] to stay – her mother being worse. Did up the work and called to Mrs. Dean's and Mr. Fenno's after dinner. Mina and I went to the woods after wintergreens.

Saturday, June 27, 1891
A cold but pleasant day. Frank went to Watkins [Glen]. I baked bread, pies, and a cake and did the Saturday's cleaning. Mina came over and I went home with her. She staid all night with me.

Sunday, June 28, 1891
A lovely day. Did up the work. Went to church and Sabbath School. Met went home with me and staid until night. Frank and Lynn went down to Chancy K---s [Kendall's]. Went to meeting this evening.

Monday, June 29, 1891
A lovely day. Did up the morning work. Washed and cleaned up this forenoon. Ma made soap and churned this forenoon. Pa went to Tyrone. Stella Mead was here this afternoon. I called to Mr. Brown's.

Tuesday, June 30, 1891
Another very pleasant day. Ironed this forenoon. Ma did the work. Pa worked on the road. Ma went to Aunt's a while this afternoon. Mina came up here. Aunt and Lola came down this evening.

Wednesday, July 1, 1891
A stormy day. I set out my plants this forenoon and churned. Orville went to Dundee. Mina and Satie and I went to Mrs. McClure's a-visiting this afternoon. Called to Mr. Brown's and Mrs. Castner's.

Thursday, July 2, 1891
A very nice day. Mr. Jansen came down after me. I went up home with him and picked thirty quarts of cherries. Mrs. Willover and Matie were here this evening to tea. Mr. & Mrs. Dilliston and Frank Bailey took dinner there.

Friday, July 3, 1891
A cloudy forenoon. We churned and baked and cleaned up this forenoon. Emma and Mina called here. Had a very hard hail and ice storm. Stones fell that measured 0.6 in circumference. Mina and I froze cream with them. Called to Mrs. Brown's.

Saturday, July 4, 1891
It looked quite stormy this morning. Mina and I made a freezer of ice cream. We went to Weston [NY] this afternoon with Wm. Townley's folks. Staid until after the fireworks. Had a lovely shower this evening.

Sunday, July 5, 1891
A dull gloomy day. Did up the morning work and went to church and Sunday School. Ma and Pa went down to Uncle Squire's. They got some cherries. Went to meeting this evening. Satie and Mina called.

Preserved Cherries

Pick off all of the stems and to every quart of fruit add one quart of sugar; mix well with the sugar and put them over a slow fire till the syrup commences to form, then put them over a hot fire and let them boil quickly for fifteen minutes, skimming it well. Put them boiling hot into stone jars, sealing them tightly.

Homemade Soap

First try out and strain the grease. This done, more than half of the work is done. The directions for making the soap are on every can of potash. You can make hard soap very nice, white and hard. Here is the recipe: Hard soap - empty the contents of the can of potash into a kettle with a quart of water. Stir it with a spoon or stick. The lye will dissolve immediately and become quite hot. Allow it to cool. Now take 6 pounds of clean grease, tallow or lard. Melt it until lukewarm; then commence pouring the cold lye into the melted grease gradually in a small stream until it is thoroughly mixed and drops from the stirrer the thickness of honey. To be properly done the stirring should continue for 10 minutes. It is then ready to pour into any mold.

If you follow this recipe closely you will not fail in getting nice soap. There is also a recipe for soft soap on each can of potash.

Monday, July 6, 1891
A pleasant day. We did not wash but put up our cherries. We had about forty quarts. Ma went up to Auntie's this afternoon. Mina & I called to Mrs. Bigelow's and into Mrs. Telle;r's. Went to bed at nine.

Tuesday, July 7, 1891
A stormy nasty day. We washed this morning and put our clothes to soak. Churned and cleaned up this forenoon. I wrote to A. Eaves [in Weston, NY] and sewed some on my tea gown. Went to bed at eight.

Wednesday, July 8, 1891
It looked quite story this morning but cleared off about noon and we have hung out our clothes. Baked bread and ginger cookies this morning. Aunt came down and we called to Vanchie's [Levanche]. I called to Trude's.

Thursday, July 9, 1891
A very fine day. Ironed this morning and then Aunt and I went down to Uncle Squire's and got some cherries. Lola staid with Ma. We got home at seven. Went to prayer meeting. There were 19 there.

Friday, July 10, 1891
A lovely day. Helped do up the morning work and then mended. Ma cleaned all the honey boxes this forenoon. After dinner Mina and I went to the woods after moss and wintergreens. Called to see Erva.

Saturday, July 11, 1891
Another splendid day. Helped do up the work and then went and got some flowers. Helped over to the church all the afternoon – helping for the festival. We took in thirteen dollars and five cents.

Sunday, July 12, 1891
A terrible warm day. Got up at six. Helped do up the morning work. Got ready and went to meeting and Sunday School. After dinner went to bed and staid until four. Aunt & Lola came down. Went to meeting this evening.

Good Girl's Cake

One cup butter, one and a half cups sugar, three eggs, one cup chopped raisins, one teaspoonful of soda dissolved in two tablespoons of milk, spice to taste, and add flour enough to roll as cookies.

Monday, July 13, 1891
A pleasant but very warm day. Washed and churned this forenoon. After dinner went over to the church and helped wash up the dishes and clean up. Called to Mrs. Dean's. She gave me a blue dress.

Tuesday, July 14, 1891
Another very warm day. Ironed this morning and then worked on my sunbonnet. Aunt & Lola came down. We went down to the mill. Lessie Parks and I called to Mr. Wintermute's.

Wednesday, July 15, 1891
A very fine day. Did up our morning work. Called to Mrs. Cole's and then got Orson some cloth for a shirt and worked on it this forenoon. After dinner went up to Warsaw. Got there at half past four. Staid to Joe's.

Thursday, July 16, 1891
A lovely day. Got up at six. After breakfast went to picking cherries. Picked forty quarts. After dinner went up to John's a few minutes & then came home. Called to Uncle Squire's. Went to prayer meeting this evening.

Friday, July 17, 1891
A very nice day. Got up at six. Helped do up the morning work. Churned and helped do up forty quarts of cherries this forenoon. Washed and cleaned up this afternoon & put down the church oil cloths.

Saturday, July 18, 1891
A stormy, nasty day. Ma and Pa went down to John's this morning. Ironed and baked bread this forenoon. Mended this afternoon. Lessie called this P.M. Mina staid with me tonight. Mrs. J. called.

Sunday, July 19, 1891
A very nice day. Did up the morning work and went to meeting and Sunday School. Mina came home with me from church. After dinner we called to Mrs. Dean's & Tina's. Went to church this evening.

Berry Corn Cake

Two cups of Indian meal, one cup of flour, three tablespoonfuls sugar, two eggs, teaspoonful of salt, teaspoonful of soda, dissoved in a pint of sour milk, or if the milk is sweet, use two teaspoonfuls of cream of tartar. To be filled with berries and baked till a nice brown.

Monday, July 20, 1891
A lovely day. Helped do up the work and wash this forenoon and went up to Auntie's a few minutes. Aunt and Lola were here this afternoon. I got me a Russian Circular. Alice Fenno called here.

Tuesday, July 21, 1891
A nice day but very warm. Helped do up the morning work and ironed a few pieces then went over to Frank Kendall's and picked berries. Picked 85 quarts. Aunt and Lola were down this afternoon.

Wednesday, July 22, 1891
Another very warm day. Helped do up the morning work and then went to picking berries. Picked 48 quarts and quit at five. Was sick. Aunty and Lola and Mrs. Dean were here this afternoon.

Thursday, July 23, 1891
A nice cool day but looked quite stormy. I did not do much of anything. Ma went a-red raspberrying this forenoon and I this afternoon. I went over to Mrs. D's. Went to prayer meeting.

Friday, July 24, 1891
A lovely day. Helped do up the morning's work and then got ready and went up to Mr. Dilliston's. Mrs. Jansen went with me. Got home a few minutes after seven. Ma washed a few things.

Saturday, July 25, 1891
A cool and very nice day. Helped do up the morning work and then went over to Frank's and picked berries. I picked 80 quarts. Ma picked this afternoon. She picked 12 quarts. Aunt and Lola were down.

Sunday, July 26, 1891
A cool and cloudy day. Helped do up the morning work and went to meeting and Sunday School. Fred took dinner with the boys. Had a thundershower. Called to Mett's & Mrs. Cole's. Went to church this evening.

Monday, July 27, 1891
A lovely day. Helped do up the morning work and then Ma and I went and picked berries for Frank Kendall. I picked 33 quarts and Ma 24 quarts. Went up to Auntie's a few minutes this evening.

Tuesday, July 28, 1891
A very nice and pleasant day. Helped do up the morning's work then picked berries this forenoon. 20 quarts. After dinner Mettie and I went up to Mr. Jansen's and got some black cherries. Ma washed this forenoon.

Wednesday, July 29, 1891
A very nice day. Looked showery all day. Helped do up the morning work and ironed some. Ma and I went over to Elia Crane's. Got home before six. Called down to Mr. Fenno's. Had a terrible thunderstorm. Mr. Jansen's barn burned.

Red Raspberry Jam

Pick them carefully, take equal quantities of berries and sugar, stir it continually put the fruit first into a saucepan, and when the water parts are evaporated add the sugar; simmer slowly for fifteen or twenty minutes.

Thursday, July 30, 1891
A stormy cloudy day but quite cool. Finished ironing this morning and churned. After dinner did some mending and then went up to Auntie's a few minutes. Sate and Mina and I went to prayer meeting.

Friday, July 31, 1891
A splendid day. Helped do up the morning work and cleaned up some. Went over to Frank's and picked berries. Picked 25 quarts. Brought home 2 quarts. Mrs. Dean spent the day with us.

Saturday, August 1, 1891
Another nice day. Helped do up the morning work and then went over and picked berries. Picked 15 quarts, Ma went up to Auntie's this afternoon. I called to Mrs. Dean's. Kate and I went up too Mr. Gregory's.

Sunday, August 2, 1891
A lovely day. Helped do up the morning work and went to meeting and Sunday School. Went home with Emma Peck. We called to Mr. Jansen's. Went to Endeavor Meeting. Was sick and did not stay to church.

Monday, August 3, 1891
A splendid day. Did up the morning work. Helped wash and then Jennie and I went a-berrying. After dinner went to work in the basket factory. Made 28 baskets. Went to the store this evening.

Tuesday, August 4, 1891
A terrible rainy and unpleasant day. Helped do up the morning work and then went to work in the factory. After supper went over to Mrs. Dean's and ground some pepper. Frank K[endall] paid me for picking berries.

Wednesday, August 5, 1891
A very nice day. Worked in the mill about two hours then went home and after dinner Mina and I went to Tyrone. Emma P[eck], Mina & Satie and Flora called here this evening.

Thursday, August 6, 1891
Another lovely day. Helped do up the morning work and then went to work in the mill. Aunt and Lola were down and spent the day. Satie, Mina and I went to prayer meeting.

Friday, August 7, 1891
A pleasant morning. Helped do up the morning work. Worked in the mill all day. Mrs. Dean called here. Rained quite hard this evening. Some sore thumbs.

Saturday, August 8, 1891
A lovely day. Helped do up the morning work and then went to work in the mill. Worked until three this P.M. then went to the ball play [ball game]. Ma and I went up to Mr. Brown's a few minutes this evening.

Sunday, August 9, 1891
A cloudy and very warm day. Helped do up the work and went to meeting and Sunday School. Jennie Bennett came home with me. We went to church this evening. Had quite a shower.

Monday, August 10, 1891
A terrible warm day. Helped do up the morning work and then went to work in the mill. It rained this afternoon. Pa went down to Tyrone. Quit work at six.

Tuesday, August 11, 1891
Had a fine shower this afternoon. Helped do up the morning work and then worked in the mill. Made 170 baskets. Emma Peck and Mina and I trimmed the Banner this evening. Went over to the church.

Wednesday, August 12, 1891
A rainy nasty day. Finished my wrapper this forenoon. Leon Clark took dinner with us. Worked in the mill this afternoon. Made 106 baskets. Went up to the store and got some rubbers.

Thursday, August 13, 1891
A cloudy forenoon but pleasant this afternoon. Worked in the factory

| Ther. | WED. AUG. 5, 1891 | Wea. |

A very nice day
worked in the mill
about two hours then
went home and after
dinner Mina and
I went to Tyrone
Emma P——, Mina &
Satie and Cora
called here this Evening

| Ther. | THURSDAY 6 | Wea. |

Another lovely day
helped do up the
morning work and
then went to work
in the Mill Aunt
and Cola were down
and spent the day
Satie, Mina and I
went to prayer meeting

all day. Satie and Mina and Jennie and I went to prayer meeting this evening. There were twenty-five present.

Friday, August 14, 1891
A lovely day but rained this evening. Finished fixing my white wrapper. Worked in the factory until seven this evening. Aunt and Lola were down a little while today.

Saturday, August 15, 1891
A cloudy morning but cleared off and a pleasant afternoon. Made baskets this forenoon and went to the Ball game & festival this afternoon and evening. Took in $14.55 clear.

Sunday, August 16, 1891
Cool this morning but very warm afternoon. Colder at night. Went to church and Sunday School this forenoon. After dinner went to bed. Amelia and children went here. I went to church this evening.

Monday, August 17, 1891
A very nice day. Helped do up the morning work and then went to work in the mill. Went up to the store. Called to Mr. Brown's and Mettie's this evening. Aunt and Lola were down today.

Tuesday, August 18, 1891
Helped do up the morning work and ironed until seven. Then went to work in the mill. Had a terrible thundershower this forenoon. After supper Satie and Edna and I washed up the church dishes.

Wednesday, August 19, 1891
Cloudy this morning but faired off and had a lovely day. Worked in the mill all day. Aunt was down a few minutes. Called to Mrs. Dean's and went down to Tyrone with Ansyl's [Ansel Littell] folks.

Thursday, August 20, 1891
A very nice day. Helped do up the morning work and then worked in the mill. Quit at five. Our hoops gave out. Ma went up to Mr. Brown's this P.M. Went to prayer meeting.

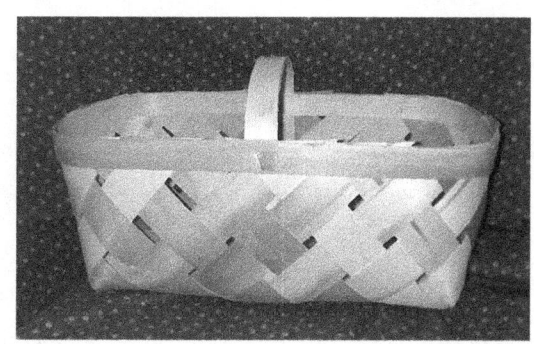

Viola did not say exactly what kind of baskets she made - but this is a typical New York State grape basket of the time. Viola lived in the middle of the Finger Lakes grape growing region.

Friday, August 21, 1891

A showery day. Helped do up the morning work. Made two cakes and a batch of ginger cookies. Aunt and Lola came down. Worked in the mill this afternoon. Made 80 baskets. Had the tooth ache all night.

Saturday, August 22, 1891

A lovely day. Helped do up the morning work and then Mr. Bigelow's and I went to Dundee. I had three teeth pulled. Hannibal and Henry and Uncle Squire went here. We went to the ball play this P.M. Players ate supper here.

Sunday, August 23, 1891

A rainy and nasty day. Went to meeting and Sunday School. Mate and George Crane were here. Henry went home with them. I went to meeting this evening.

Monday, August 24, 1891

A lovely forenoon but showery this afternoon. Did up the morning work and then worked in the Factory. Made 180 baskets. Mrs. Corey came over here.

Tuesday, August 25, 1891

A lovely day. Helped do up the morning work and then went to work in the mill. Made 210 baskets. Aunt and Lola came down tonight. I went up to Mrs. Cole's a few minutes.

Wednesday, August 26, 1891
Cloudy this morning but pleasant after. Satie and I trimmed the banner. Went to Shepard's grove to a picnic. Had a lovely time. Got home at five. Went up to Auntie's, Mrs. Corey staid there.

Thursday, August 27, 1891
A very nice day but quite warm. Helped do up the morning's work then went to work in the Factory. Made 200 baskets. Ma went up to Stella Price's this afternoon. I went to prayer meeting.

Friday, August 28, 1891
Another nice day. Cooler and wind. Did not feel very well this morning but went to work and made 203 baskets. Felt better this afternoon. Pa went down to Uncle Squire's. I called to Mrs. Dean's this evening.

Saturday, August 29, 1891
A cold day but quite pleasant. Helped do up the morning work and then went to work in the mill. Made 200 baskets. Mrs. Corey and Aunt and Lola called. Satie & Mina, Lessie, and I went up to the hall.

Sunday, August 30, 1891
A pleasant but cold day. Helped do up the morning work. Went to Meeting and Sunday School. After dinner, Ma and I went up to Aunt Mate's. She came home with us. Went to the Lecture this evening.

Monday, August 31, 1891
A pleasant but cool day. Helped do up the morning work and ironed a few pieces then went to work in the factory and made 200 baskets. Aunt and Lola were down here a little while. Had a shower this afternoon.

Tuesday, September 1, 1891
A very pleasant day. Helped do up the morning work and ironed a few pieces then went to work in the mill. Made 205 baskets. Ma and I called down to Johnnie Gregory's this evening.

Wednesday, September 2, 1891
A cool morning and cloudy but cleared off and had a lovely day. Helped do up the morning work and then worked in the mill. Made 210 baskets. Ma and I went to Auntie's calling.

Thursday, September 3, 1891
A pleasant day. Helped do up the morning work then went to work in the mill. Made 210 baskets. Aunt and Lola were down. Satie & Mina and I went to prayer meeting. Rained this evening.

Friday, September 4, 1891
A nice day but not very warm. Helped do up the morning work and

then worked in the mill all day. Made 190 baskets. Called to Mrs. Dean's this evening. Aunt and Lola were here this evening.

Saturday, September 5, 1891
A cloudy nasty rainy day. Helped do up the morning work. Went to work in the mill. Made 220 baskets. Aunt and Lola were down a little while this afternoon.

Sunday, September 6, 1891
A lovely day. Helped do up the morning work and then went to meeting and Sunday School. After meeting went up to Auntie's to dinner. We called to Mr. Brown's and Mrs. Teller's. Went to meeting this evening.

Monday, September 7, 1891
Another very nice day. Helped do up the morning work and then worked in the mill. Made 235 baskets. Ironed this evening. A tombstone agent staid here all night. Aunt & Lola were down a while.

Tuesday, September 8, 1891
A lovely day. Helped do up the morning work and then went to work in the mill. Made 235 baskets. Aunt and Lola were down a few minutes this evening. Claude and agent took dinner.

Wednesday, September 9, 1891
A heavy frost this morning but a very fair day. Helped do up the morning work. Did not go to work until after ten. Made 155 baskets. Jennie & I called down to Mr. Young's this evening.

Thursday, September 10, 1891
A very nice day. Pa went to Wayne [NY] after hoops for Mr. Lamb this morning. Jennie and I went elderberrying. Pa went up to Mr. Jansen's to the raisin [raising? – maybe barn raising] this afternoon. I did not work in the mill.

Friday, September 11, 1891
A lovely day. Did not work in the mill. Ma and Pa went down to Thannie Peoples's[?] to a surprise party for Aunt Isabelle. Jennie and I went up to Mr. Jansen's a little while this evening.

| Ther. | TUES. SEPT. 8, 1891 | Wea. |

A lovely day helped
do up the morning
work and then went
to work in the mill
made 235 Baskets
Aunt and Lola were
down a few minutes
this evening Claud &
I went to [?] dinner

| Ther. | WEDNESDAY 9 | Wea. |

A heavy frost this
morning but a very
fair day helped do
up the morning work
did not go to work
until after ten made
155 Baskets Jennie
and I called down to
Mr Young's this Evening

Saturday, September 12, 1891
A very fine day. Helped do up the morning work and then went to work in the mill. Made 125 baskets. Hoops give out. Pa went to Watkins [Glen]. Ma and Pa went over to Elias's. Mina staid with me.

Sunday, September 13, 1891
Looked rainy all day but not rain to amount to much. Did up the morning work and went to church. Ansyl ate dinner with us. Ma and Pa came home tonight.

Monday, September 14, 1891
A nice day. Helped do up the morning work and then went to work in the mill. Made 170 baskets. Aunt came down and we all called to Mrs. Dean's. Satie was up a few minutes.

Tuesday, September 15, 1891
A nice day but looked rainy by spells. Worked in the mill. Made 155 baskets. Mrs. Dean took dinner with us. Mrs. Jansen and I called to Trude's this evening.

Wednesday, September 16, 1891
Looked very rainy this morning but cleared off and had a lovely day. Went over to Mr. Wixon's to the Centennial. Had a lovely time. Aunt and Lola were here a while this evening.

Thursday, September 17, 1891
A very warm and sultry day. Helped do up the morning work and then worked in the mill. Made 190 baskets. Mina and I called to Mrs. Cole's. Went to prayer meeting.

Friday, September 18, 1891
A terrible warm day. Helped do up the morning work then went to work in the mill. Made 220 baskets. After supper went down and trimmed my baskets. Aunt & Lola were down a few minutes.

Saturday, September 19, 1891
Cloudy this morning but cleared off and had a lovely [day]. Went down

to Glenora to a picnic with the Reading Center Y.P.S.C.E [Young People's Society for Christian Endeavor]. Had a lovely time. John and Rose and Emma came here tonight.

Sunday, September 20, 1891
A heavy frost this morning. Did up the work. Rose, Emma, Pa and I wnt to church. Called to Auntie's. After dinner Rose, John and I called to Mrs. Cole's. Aunt, & Uncle, Edd & Nellie called here this afternoon.

Monday, September 21, 1891
A lovely day but very warm. Helped wash and churn this forenoon. After dinner went to work in the mill. Made 110 baskets. Ma and Emma went up to Aunt Mate's and spent the afternoon.

Tuesday, September 22, 1891
Another very warm day. Helped do up the morning work and then took Emma to Dundee. Staid all day. Aunt Isabelle came home with me. Had a lovely time. Came home with the sick headache.

Wednesday, September 23, 1891
A very warm but pleasant day. Helped do up the morning work. Aunt Isabelle and I peared [pared] the peaches & Ma canned them. Made baskets this P.M. After supper took Aunt down to Uncle Squire's.

Thursday, September 24, 1891
Got home this morning at half-past six. Helped do up the morning work. Pa went to Penn Yan to the Fair. I made 155 baskets. Mina and I went to Prayer meeting this evening. Terrible warm.

Friday, September 25, 1891
A very warm day. Helped do up the morning work and then made baskets about three quarters of the day. Hunt [probably J. E. Hunt] and Amos [probably Littell] were there to dinner. Aunt & Lola were down. I called to Mrs. Teller's.

Pickled Peaches

Nine pounds of peaches, three pounds of sugar, three quarts good cider vinegar. Peel the peaches, put two cloves in each peach, then put them with the sugar and vinegar in a porcelain-lined kettle; cook from five to ten minutes. Add a little whole allspice.

Ther.	SAT. SEPT. 26, 1891	Wea.

A lovely day helped do up the Saturday work Pa went to B— Stream after Peaches did not get any went to Church meeting this P.M. Came home found Ona sick Verta was here

Ther.	SUNDAY 27	Wea.

A terrible warm day helped do up the morning work and then called to Aunties Lola & her were sick went to Church after dinner called to Mr Fenno's Myra and I went to Church to night

Saturday, September 26, 1891
A lovely day. Helped do up the Saturday's work. Pa went to R[ock] Stream after peaches. Did not get any. Went to church meeting the P.M. Came home. Found Ma sick. Tina was here.

Sunday, September 27, 1891
A terrible warm day. Helped do up the morning work and then called to Auntie's. Lola and her were sick. Went to church. After dinner called to Mr. Fenno's. Mina and I went to church tonight.

Monday, September 28, 1891
A lovely day. Helped do up the morning work and then helped do the washing and cleaning up. Work in the mill this afternoon. Went up and staid all night with Aunt & Lola.

Tuesday, September 29, 1891
Another very nice day but quite windy. Pa went after peaches. Staid until after nine then went to work in the mill. Went over to Trude's a few minutes this evening.

Wednesday, September 30, 1891
A cold morning but warmer this afternoon. Helped do up the morning work and then went to work in the mill. Aunt and Lola were down this afternoon. Called up to Mrs. Teller's.

Thursday, October 1, 1891
A very lovely day. Cold this morning so we did not work in the mill until after nine. Jennie staid here and helped Ma pear [pare] peaches. Mr. Lamb took us girls down to Tyrone this evening.

Friday, October 2, 1891
Another nice day. Helped do up the morning work and then went to work in the mill. Ma went up to Auntie's a few minutes. Satie, Mina, Jennie & I went to Tyrone this evening.

Saturday, October 3, 1891
A terrible warm weather day. Helped do up the work then worked in

the mill. Pa went to Watkins. Mr. Lamb took a load down to Tyrone. I was sick and went to Mr. Murray's and laid down until I came home.

Sunday, October 4, 1891
Another terrible warm day. Do not feel any better. Edith, Eunice, Satie, Mina, Jennie, Edna, Nina called here. Orson went after the Dr. this evening. Aunt and Lola were down this afternoon.

Monday, October 5, 1891
Rained a little this morning. Am feeling a little better. The Dr. came up this morning. Ma washed the colored clothes. Aunt and Lola were down this afternoon. Mrs. Teller and Jennie were here this evening.

Tuesday, October 6, 1891
[No entry.]

Wednesday, October 7, 1891
[No entry.]

Thursday, October 8, 1891
Dr. Mottram came this morning and staid until in the afternoon sometime.

Friday, October 9, 1891
[No entry.]

Saturday, October 10, 1891
Dr. Harvey was here for a Counsel this morning.

[No more entries for October or November.]

Monday, December 7, 1891
Mrs. Dean died this afternoon at half-past two.

Wednesday, December 8, 1891
[No entry.]

Thursday, December 9, 1891

Mrs. Dean's funeral was here at the church this forenoon at eleven.

Friday, December 10, 1891

Went outdoors for the first time this morning. Went down to Mr. Fenno's. It was a lovely day.

[No more entries. End of diary.]

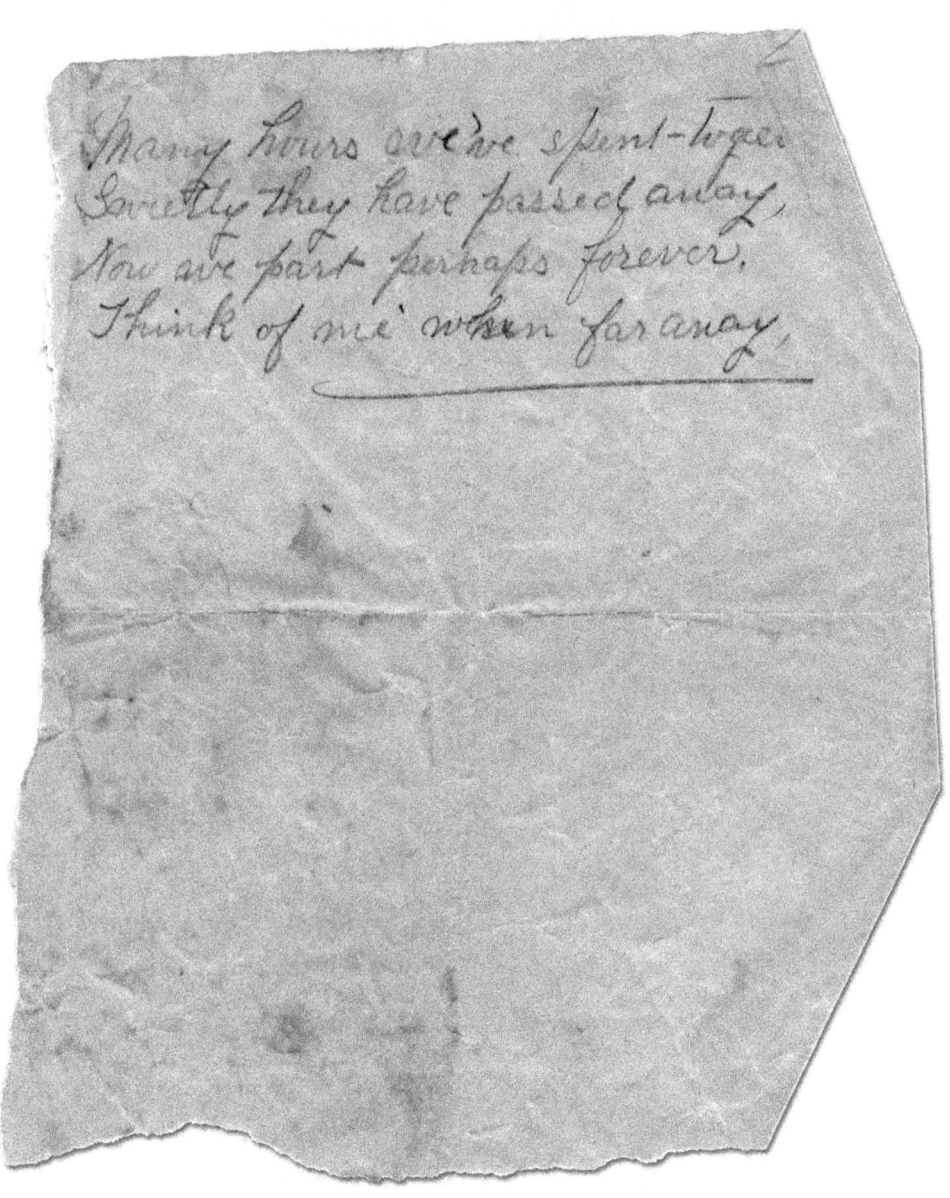

A poem found in the back pocket of Viola's diary:

Many hours we've spent together
Sweetly they have passed away.
Now we part perhaps forever,
Think of me when far away.

Afterward

After the end of this diary, Viola Coolbaugh became Mrs. Edward Littell on December 19, 1892 and eventually moved to Dundee, New York. Edward was a contractor who specialized in concrete work. They had no children. Viola had a lake house in Starkey that burned to the ground after a spark from a passing New York Central train started a fire in 1909. Viola's beloved Aunt Mate [Mary Force] died in Viola's home in Dundee of appendicitus in 1911.

Viola lived to be eighty-years-old and died at the Hillgate nursing home in Dundee, New York on September 28, 1954.

Viola Coolbaugh Littell is buried in Altay Baptist Church cemetery.

Bibliography

Austin, Susan Rockwell. "Tyrone Union Cem., Schuyler co., NY--p1." 1999. RootsWeb. 10 October 2009 <http://www.rootsweb.ancestry.com/~nyschuyl/tyuncem1.htm >.

Cleveland, Stafford C. *History & Directory of Yates Co., Vol 1.*, 1873.

"Hillside Cemetery, Dundee, NY." 12 October 2009 <http://74.125.93.132/search?q=cache:yc7Rqce5oHsJ:www.usgennet.org/usa/ny/county/yates/ceme/hillsidecemeCD.htm+%22john+coolbaugh%22+altay&cd=1&hl=en&ct=clnk&gl=us&client=safari >.

Howard, Helena. "Altay Cem., Tyrone, Schuyler co., NY.". 1999. RootsWeb. 10 April 2010 <http://64.233.169.104/search?q=cache:x3MTUnAgdIsJ:www.rootsweb.ancestry.com/~nyschuyl/altay.htm+littell+altay,+ny&hl=en&ct=clnk&cd=5&gl=us&client=safari>.

"Jenkins Case Won't Be Tried." *Rochester Democrat and Chronicle*, 08 May 1909: page 3.

"Mrs. Frank Force." *Rochester Democrat and Chronicle*, 11 October 1911: page 7.

"Old Fulton NY Post Cards." 02 March 2010 <http://fultonhistory.com/Fulton.html>.

Reference business directory of Schuyler County, N.Y. 1893-'94 : with map. Syracuse, NY: E. M. Child, 1893.

Schuyler County Historical Society. *Schuyler County, New York - History & Family*: Turner Publishing, 2005.

"Schuyler." *Rochester Democrat and Chronicle,* 22 December 1892 : page 4.

US GenNet. 12 October 2009 <http://74.125.93.132/search?q=cache:yc7Rqce5oHsJ:www.usgennet.org/usa/ny/county/yates/ceme/hillsidecemeCD.htm+%22john+coolbaugh%22+altay&cd=1&hl=en&ct=clnk&gl=us&client=safari >.

US GenWeb. 16 September 2009 <http://files.usgwarchives.net/ny/yates/obits/c/coolbaugh-johnw.txt3>.

More *Learning From History* publications from
New York History Review Press

A Darned Good Time
by Miss Lucy Potter, 1868

*My Centennial Diary - A Year in the Life of a
Country Boy* by Earll K. Gurnee, 1876

My Story - A Year in the Life of a Country Girl
by Ida Burnett, 1880

Upcoming

Queen City Adventure
by Emma Latier, 1902

www.ingramcontent.com/pod-product-compliance
Lightning Source LLC
Chambersburg PA
CBHW051712040426
42446CB00008B/841